Rolanda McDuffie
On
Living Life As Intended

Copyright © 2022 Rolanda McDuffie. All rights reserved. This book may not be reproduced in whole or in part without written permission from the publisher, except by a reviewer who may quote brief passages in a review; nor may any part of this book be reproduced, stored in retrieval system, or transmitted in any form or by any means, electronic, mechanical, photocopying, recording, or other, without prior written permission from the publisher.

Other books by Ersula K Odom:
At Sula's Feet
The Doris Ross Reddick Story
Miss Lizzy's Story
African Americans of Tampa
Pamala McCoy - A Shero's Story
Create Your Signature Book In A Weekend
Rogers Park Golf Course
Celebrating Tanya Martin Pekel

ISBN-978-1-7365717-4-3 Paperback

Printed and bound in the United States of America
August 2022

Published by
Sula Too Publishing
Tampa, Florida
www.sulatoo.com/publishing

Rolanda McDuffie

on

Living Life As Intended

As told to

Ersula K Odom

Sula Too Publishing

In This Book

I Am	11
In the Beginning	12
Breaking Free	15
Conditioned For Change	18
Heart Stopping Moment	21
How Could It Be?	29
Coping	31
Living	34
People	44
Life Lessons	48
Life As Intended	53
What The Future Holds For Me	55
What I Will Do	56
What I Will Change	60
What I Will Stop	62
What I Will Add?	64
About The Author	67

Ersula K Odom

Dedicated to

All of you wonderful people who continue to make life worth living

Ersula K Odom

A Tiny Book
By Sula Too Publishing

Sula Too Publishing Tiny Books offer stories of people and organizations spotlighting formative and celebrative moments that birth inspiration. Tiny Books give the reader a personal and professional peek into the subject's life, answering what, when and most often why.

The books have a similar look and feel, yet they are all very different. They offer comfort to those who see themselves in the stories and wisdom to those who find the stories unfamiliar.

Tiny Books are designed to give the subject a means of releasing top-of-mind information that's on a loop in their heads about those heartfelt events, emotions, and actions that they deem important or that they are most proud.

Your response to this Tiny Book may encourage an author to write a complete biography or inspire an autobiography where the rest of the story can be told.

This narrative applies to you as reader as well. Your story also needs to be told and now is the time. Your story is our history.

Ersula K Odom

*Living
Life As Intented*

I Am

My "I am" was so simple until the day I heard words I never would, or even could have imagined.

First, currently I work with for-profit, small business owners, and nonprofit organizations to help them become financially fit. I do this using accounting, tax, and business advisory services. I'm passionate about helping organizations and businesses understand their financial numbers. I want them to grow their business and profit so that they can create jobs and build up our economy even more.

Ersula K Odom

In the Beginning

My introduction to accounting came as a King High School 11th grader when I took an elective accounting course.

The first half of the year, I was one of two people who embraced the concepts because they clicked. They made sense to me. I felt I was onto something and decided to take it to another level.

I took accounting for a second term and that's when I realized it was something that I really enjoyed. I could see myself doing it for the rest of my life.

Maintaining this vision was not so easy. My mother and I were at my mother's friend's house when she asked me what would be major when I attend college. I replied I wanted to major in accounting. My mom laughed, and said, "That's the dumbest thing I've ever heard."

That hurt my feelings. But once I got into the business world, I realized most people don't understand what accounting is, and what it entails. I came to realize that when my mother made that hurtful statement, she just didn't understand what was involved. In her mind, accounting was just accounts payable and doing payroll.

With that thought she also told me, "I'm not paying for you to go to college to be an accountant." Yes, that's what she said. Because she thought that if I was just going to be doing payroll or accounts payable, I could just go work at a company and learn that. I did not need to get a four-year degree.

Rolanda McDuffie On Living Life As Intended

Breaking Free

Against my mother's will, I decided to pursue an accounting degree. She truly felt it was the dumbest she'd ever heard. I enrolled at North Carolina Agriculture and Technical State University. Aggie Pride! The tour I took during my high school senior year impressed me. It was one of the top schools in the country.

As for HBCUs (Historically Black Colleges & Universities), I knew that I needed to get completely away from my home state schools to increase my chances of graduating.

I knew I didn't need to be at either FAMU (Florida Agricultural & Mechanical University) in Tallahassee,

Florida with my friends or at Bethune in Daytona Florida with some of my other friends. I needed to just get away. I enrolled at North Carolina Agriculture and Technical State University.

I have nothing against the great parties I am sure I would have attended, if surrounded by my childhood friends. Now, don't get me wrong, A&T knew how to throw a good party, but it was not as easy to lose focus when I had to build new relationships.

It's different when you are in a new environment and must build relationships before being invited anywhere. I felt would been different at FAMU, or Florida State, with my friends calling me saying, "Hey, girl, I got a party over here." I would've been everywhere! I decided that being surrounded by life time friends probably was not the best for me. Therefore, I attended a school away from my home state.

Ersula K Odom

Conditioned For Change

During my senior year in high school, my mother actually moved to Charlotte North Carolina. Even though I was in Greensboro, we were still a little over an hour apart.

College was a difficult adjustment, but not due to moving, we did that all the time.

When I was growing up we moved at least every two years, meaning I was always having to meet new people, gain new friends, build new relationships anyway.

The reason we moved so often was due to my mother's determination to survive. She was a single mother who worked really hard. She wasn't on any form of public assistance, even though my father didn't pay child support. To be honest, she struggled to raise my brother and me by herself.

More often than not, relocating was financially motivated. One day she would say something like, "I can't. This isn't going to work out. We've got to find a new place to live." And that was that.

I remember going to Atlanta to stay for a summer in between my eighth and ninth grade year and when I came back home after this summer was over we had moved. I did not know about it until we were going in a different direction from our other home and I asked the question I was told that we have moved.

Moving to a different part of town might as well have been to a different state. Because it caused me to leave one school and go to a new and unfamiliar school.

Rolanda McDuffie On Living Life As Intended

Heart Stopping Moment

In 2017, I discovered I had skin cancer. That was mind blowing and a complete mental shift. It was a situation where all of my life I've been sun adverse. Whenever I am outside, I'm always looking for the closest shade tree.

Because I was never one who liked being in the sun, it was hard for me to understand how something like that could happen to me.

This news brought me face to face with my mortality and the reality I had no control over it. I couldn't control what was happening at that moment nor what caused the condition.

If I had been the type of person who

would lay out in the sun, it would be a little bit easier to understand and accept. But because I had never, I mean never been one to seek sun rays, "How could I've avoided this?"

Getting past that... I heard the word cancer and I, like anyone else, I was scared. Then hearing my doctors say that there was a nine out of ten percent chance that it's going to come back a few times in my lifetime. This was based on the fact that I was so young and my body was exposed to a consistent amount of sunlight.

Knowing that it's a possibility that if it does come back, I could possibly die within six to eight weeks of getting it was traumatizing.

Rolanda McDuffie On Living Life As Intended

I told the doctor, "We need talk about this." I objected, holding on to a universal perception that dark skinned people don't get skin cancer.

I have to thank my having thyroid issues, which I learned about in college, for uncovering this condition.

Thyroid caused me to have dry patchy areas of skin. During a routine examination I drew the doctor's attention to what I had treated as just another dry patchy area of skin that was a little different.

I always used a thicker lotion to get rid of dry areas, whether it's Lubriderm or Aveeno with oatmeal. This particular time, I followed my normal routine, but it didn't quite go away. I rationalized that I wasn't using the lotion as often as I should have.

The dry patch turned into a sore, and then the sore scabbed a little, but the scar never healed. It became callous. Then it started. The callousness started got thicker and thicker, and was rising. I peeled off the callous and it returned to an open wound. The scab came back. It calloused again. I did it again, took the callousness off, peeled it off, and then it happened again.

After nine months of this I said, "Okay, I need to go to the dermatologist because something's not right."

It was my dermatologist who uttered the words, "It looks like you may have skin cancer."

I challenged her with "What are you talking about? Black people don't get skin cancer."

She looked at me kind of funny. I asked, "What!" "Stop playing, doc." She did a biopsy. About four or five days later, a nurse called me. Over the phone, she said, "Hey, Rolanda, how are you? I have your results back." She said, "Hold on." She put the phone down

When she came back, honestly, I don't know what I was expecting her to say. When she said, "Your results came back positive that you do have skin cancer, yada, yada, yada." She just went on this long spiel of stuff that I was incapable of hearing.

I don't know what she said because I was stuck on the word "cancer". I stopped her with, "Hold on, time out, flag on the play. I don't know what you're talking about, lady."

Because we don't have these conversations in my family, what she said about there being two types cancer, just led to questions. I asked, "I don't know what that means. Is that good? Is that bad?

She explained, the type of skin cancer I had was Squamous cell carcinoma. However, I was told that the skin cancer can come back in any of the three forms (Squamous cell carcinoma, Basal cell cancer or melanoma). So, although I did not have the deadliest form, which is melanoma, I could still get it in the future.

What are you talking about?" That was literally my response to her.

Then funny thing that I found out was there's only one black dermatologist in the state of Florida. He was not my doctor, but I met him later at a networking event and I shared my story with him.

They decided to cut the cancer out, because they didn't want to radiate. I was told, that when they apply radiation to that area, it generally comes back within 20 years. Thus, they generally don't offer it to younger people because they don't want it to come back. Older people, they assume that they're going to pass away and it won't be an issue. So radiation is most used as a treatment for older patients.

When I walked in to the plastic surgeon's office for him to cut it out, he was looking at my chart. He looked at me, looked down at my chart, looked at me again, he looked down at my chart, he looked at me again, and he looked at my chart. He was mesmerized.

He finally said, "What the...In all the years that I've been practicing, I've never seen this before."

I asked, "What are you saying?" He said, "Generally speaking, when someone your complexion comes into my office and they have skin cancer, they're twice your age. If they're your age, then they have much fairer complexion."

He continued, "This is unbelievable for me....I've never...Wow!" It was even a shocker for him.

When I met the black doctor he said he wished that I had reached him earlier because he would have written an adjunct paper about me at the University of South Florida (USF). My condition was so unlikely and it was not normal.

Our conversation was full of questions. What's the synopsis version? What did they surmised happened? Do you have a white parent that you don't know about or something?

Both of parents are dark skinned like me. It's not something that anyone in my family has ever had.

Rolanda McDuffie On Living Life As Intended

How Could It Be?

Until now, I have rarely shared my skin cancer journey. At one point I posted something about it on Facebook to a handful of people. I focused more on skin care awareness than my personal situation. I posted, "Hey, I went through this, so I want everybody to be cautious."

That post was almost a year and a half after the diagnosis. Only about 10 people knew what was really happening. I stopped sharing because a few people told me, "You probably don't really have it." Or, "Don't say that."

Upon hearing about me having skin cancer, friends and family would often down play it' or say, "The doctor just told you that to get additional billable hours."

I felt as though most people don't take skin cancer as being as important as a breast cancer. I'm not trying to put one above the other, but at the end of the day, cancer is cancer. It could take you out regardless of what it is. I think that's why I shied away from telling my story. Even though telling my story could possibly save lives.

Especially since other conditions may be confused with cancer if based on description alone. For example psoriasis could be described as dry patchy skin. They look the same and act the same, but the difference is, it never healed.

Also, skin cancer for African-Americans looks totally different from skin cancer of non-African-Americans. The way it shows up for us is different.

The doctor shared that often we get skin cancer on the bottom of our foot, which is really strange. Sometimes is appears on our head and hidden beneath our hair. That makes it silent and invisible. So we don't notice.

Ersula K Odom

Coping

New questions. What's your regimen? Now, what are you going to do to maintain health in this area?

Per the doctor, if I'm ever out in the sun for eight hours or more, I need to wear sunscreen. That was another question that challenged my reality.

I had no idea what SPF meant. I questioned, "Do I want a high number or low number? What do you do with it?" I had no clue. "Do I want a 10? Do I want 100?" I had no idea. Answer - I need to wear SPF of at least 70 or more.

However, I'm never in the sun for that long unless I'm on vacation. So, when I'm on vacation and I'm in the sun for an extended period of time, then yes, I will wear it.

Honestly, it's hard for me to even remember on a daily basis. I know that sounds weird, but when you spend your whole life not thinking about sunscreen, it's hard to start routinely using it.

But again, if I know that I'm going to be in the sun for four hours or more, I wear sunscreen. I don't know what else to change because, like I said, I naturally avoid the sun.

As for coping with this, my training may have started as a child. I have scars on my face and a birthmark. I was bullied and it was emotionally painful. Even before the "bullying" started, I remember kids staring at me all the time. I couldn't help but be self-conscious.

How do I survive this? How did I become the "wonderful person" that I am since I was bullied and had difficult issues?

I just kept pushing. Although I've never thought I was the prettiest, I liked to laugh and have a good time. That was the way I built friendships and relationships. I was funny without being the class clown.

I used to talk a lot. Even so, my mother didn't know the pain and hurt that her child was going through.

As an adult, I briefly shared my experiences with my mother. She was shocked and she said, "I never knew that." We never had a full conversation about it.

As a kid, honestly, she was never present enough for me to have that conversation because, she worked two or three jobs, and so she was at work most of the time. When she was at home, she was tired or aggravated. I didn't have the opportunity to talk about it. I just dealt with it.

It became my nature that when life bullies me, I just deal with.

Ersula K Odom

Living

I've always been interested in traveling, and I've been traveling for some time.

When I learned I had skin cancer and was wading through that whole mental processing thing, I had to sit and I ask myself if I felt I had done everything that I wanted to do before I died. And my answer was no. And I had to ask myself, "Why not? What are you waiting on?"

I think a lot of times, for me, it was waiting for someone else to do it with, whether it was friends, or a guy I was dating.

It was always, "I don't have anybody to do it with. More often than not, when

I asked somebody, they didn't want to go.

I came to realize that I had to stop waiting on anybody to do anything and just do it. It became plainly clear that when it's my time, it's my time. I started doing more solo traveling and just saying, "You know what? Forget it. I'm just going to go."

I had a new mission, making sure I've done everything that I want to do while I am here, while I have time to do it. Travel was on the top of that list of things that I always wanted to do. So I travel. A lot.

I've been to South Africa, which is number one in by book , my favorite, as well as Kenya. I've been to Cuba,

Iceland, Paris, London, and Rome.

When COVID-19 hit in 2020, I had just returned to the United States from Columbia, New Mexico, Costa Rica, Dominican Republic, Jamaica, Bahamas, and the Cayman Islands.

I've also been to Canada.

I'm often asked about how I function in places where I don't speak their language? Google Translate is my best friend. Google Translate and Google Maps are the top two most used apps on my phone when I'm out of the country. For sure and they work quite well, if I may add.

Software was also a huge factor in my getting over the fear of international travel and not being able to speak the language or thinking you can't get around because you can. It really is a lot simpler than most people imagine.

What I also found of late is that it's cheaper to travel out of the country than it has been to travel inside the country, which I find very strange. But, it has been the case. The three times I went to Africa my tickets were less than $650.

I believe the first time I went to South Africa, it was $535. It was a crazy trip because I knew I wanted to go to Johannesburg, Durban, and Cape Town. When I first started checking for flights between the two, they were about $90 one way, which really isn't bad.

For some reason, that night, I didn't buy my ticket. I was online, but I put the tablet down and I totally forgot about it.

About a week before I was supposed to leave, I remembered. "Oh, crap, I didn't get my tickets to fly in-between these cities." I went online that night and it wouldn't allow me to purchase a ticket because they were having a sale

I had to wait until after midnight, and then it was like a raffle type scenario. Whenever your number came up, the system allowed you to get on the site and purchase the tickets. I was so happy that I waited because my ticket between Johannesburg and Cape town was $11, with a $6 baggage fee!

Between Durban and Cape Town, it was $9. I was stunned.

Let's be clear, you can't advise people to do that, because you can get stuck. That happened to be the luck of the draw for me because the tickets were originally about $90. If it had been, I would not have complained.

Ersula K Odom

People

I've met quite a few interesting people during my travels and they often ask if I get lonely traveling alone.

I found that I prefer solo traveling because when you travel in groups, you tend to only speak to those individuals in your group. You're not really engaged with people outside of your group unless you're buying something or asking questions.

When you're traveling solo, people will open up to other people, and they will open up to you. I've been able to find out more about other cultures because I'm speak one-on-one to someone who is local. It is a mutual benefit for they have questions about America as well.

Rolanda McDuffie On Living Life As Intended

I find that it becomes an engaging experience instead of watching a country go by from a tour bus window.

I enjoy being free to move and go as you please. You don't have to worry about what other people want or don't want to do, or what they can't financially do. It's a matter of just being you when you want to be you.

I truly enjoyed this kind of freedom when I went to Kenya. I didn't even take pictures or film because I was focused on "giving back." I didn't feel like taking pictures was something that I needed. I do wish I had taken a picture for my private collection.

There was a grandmother with six grandchildren. The mother and father had been killed, and the grandmother was raising the children.

They had a farm. But there was a problem. In order to send the six kids to school, the grandmother needed to buy them clothes, and shoes, and give them supplies, but she didn't have a way to make any money. So, there's a program in Kenya that will allow you to purchase pigs for grandmothers.

They mate the pig with other pigs. Of course, then came these little baby pigs that they either sold to make money, or raised to later give away or eat.

I bought the grandmother a pig and she was really grateful. I was able to meet the children and spend some time with them. They sang this song and they danced. The grandmother fed me. They didn't have very much food, but she was so thankful that she was trying to give me what little they had. That really touched my spirit.

Those kinds of experiences are what I look forward to when I travel. I love being able to meet and understand people and their native culture.

What I found is that we're all different, but we're all the same. That's what I found in my travels.

Ersula K Odom

Life Lessons

I've learned to be more accepting of people. When I see that people are down, I try to be more considerate of people for who they are and what they're going through. When they have issues, I try to be more open to being there to discuss it.

When I'm home in the Tampa Bay Area, that feeling of giving back is replicated by helping businesses. My passion is helping business owners understand their numbers so that they can grow their businesses.

Having the opportunity to present for organizations such as the Women's Business Center and the Small Business Development Center allows me to help those business owners that may be struggling with their finances. I can help them better understand why their accounting is important.

What most business owners don't realize is their accounting tells the story of what's really going on in their business. That is if they're truly recording their transactions the way that they should.

A lot of times, it's helping them understand, first, that they need to be recording their financial transactions so that they can get a better idea of where their business has been and where it's going. Owners often think, "I have money in my bank account, so we're good."

Once I get them to understand I say, "Okay, now we have to keep track of these finances." Then I can show them how to keep track of them. Then they're able to see it and say, "Okay, this is where I'm falling short.... I need to cut some expenses here to increase my profit."

Maybe the sale price or the price that I put on my product is not high enough to cover my cost, so now, I need to increase the price of my product so that I can now make a profit going forward."

Those are some ways that I help business owners because some business owners will just get into business and they'll look at their competitors and see what they're charging, and they try to do the same thing.

But the business owners understand what's going on behind the scenes with their competitors. The competitor may not even be making money based on the price that they're charging, or they may have systems that allow them to cut their costs better than you can.

If you blindly follow a competitor by assuming what they're doing is something you can copy, a lot of times, business owners end up getting that wrong.

I assist business owners with their cash flow management. That way, I am proud to say that I've helped some business owners who were on the verge of going out of business to get their cash flow in order. It helped them to survive the going-out-of-business storm.

Until you get your finances in order and are able to track them, you'll never know what you can do or what changes you can make in order to stay in business or to make a profit.

Rolanda McDuffie On Living Life As Intended

Life As Intended

I have a piece of artwork on my wall that I wake up to, and it says, 'Live the life you imagined.' That is my goal now. I aim to live the life I imagine.

When I saw it, I said, "That's it." Because I don't see anyone doing that or advising other to live their lives as intended, I had to garner my inspiration from a piece of art. It had been waiting for me to need it.

The way that I see myself living my life the way that I imagine now is as a successful CPA accounting firm that offers consulting services to business owners. I want my business to evolve into a business that allows me to travel internationally and see the world, experience different cultures, but still be there for my clients and provide the level of service that they require.

Living as intended is to wake up and to do those things that make me happy. It's to live stress-free, and to love my family and friends, and for them to love me the same way.

That's the life that I imagine.

What The Future Holds For Me

I plan to focus on my ideal clients, and grow my ideal client base. My goal, for my business, is to be more a consulting-based business and less compliance based. To offer less transaction processing and offer more consulting to business owners so that they can grow their business.

I want to create virtual business such that when I decide to travel, it's not an issue. I want to maintain my client base and work with them, even while I'm traveling abroad.

So there, I still and will always have goals. That is how my live is intended. As I embrace my client responsibility,

I am free to be me.

Rolanda McDuffie On Living Life As Intended

What are my Living Life As Intended Must Do Items?

Ersula K Odom

*What I Will Do
to live my life as intended?*

Rolanda McDuffie On Living Life As Intended

Ersula K Odom

*What I Will Change
such that I can
live my life as intended*

Rolanda McDuffie On Living Life As Intended

Ersula K Odom

*What I Will Stop
such that I can
live my life as intended?*

Rolanda McDuffie On Living Life As Intended

Ersula K Odom

*What I Will Add
Such that I can
live my life as intended?*

Rolanda McDuffie On Living Life As Intended

About The Author

Rolanda S. McDuffie

Rolanda S. McDuffie, CPA is a native of Tampa, Florida. She graduated from King High School where she was first introduced to the field of accounting. She went on to attend North Carolina Agricultural & Technical University. At NCA&T she earned a Bachelor's degree in Accounting. Ms. McDuffie continued her education by obtaining an MBA and Master's in Accounting & Finance as well.

Ms. McDuffie manages a successful CPA firm which she started over eight years ago. Her professional passion is to see small business owners and non-profit organizations grow and become financially fit through the use of accounting, tax, investing and business advisory services. That same passion is what drives her to serve the community in various, related capacities. Ms. McDuffie is frequently called upon to provide her expertise at workshops, seminars, and conferences. She currently serves on the Board of Directors of several non-profit organizations and is a member of the Mayor's

African American Advisory Council for the City of Tampa.

While Ms. McDuffie certainly enjoys her profession, she understands the importance of balancing life with leisure activities. Her love of travel has taken her to South Africa, England, Italy, China, Iceland, Cuba, Kenya and France to name a few. In addition to travel, she enjoys live music, movies, fine dining, and adventurous excursions. Her incredible sense of humor helps her to not take her golf game (or lack thereof) too seriously.

Rolanda McDuffie On Living Life As Intended

Ersula K Odom

Ersula K. Odom is CEO of Sula Too LLC, founder of Recuing History, Inc., publisher, legacy wall designer, legacy writer, and living history performer.

Ersula's publishing company was born from her desire highlight extraordinary stories by average and ordinary people.

Her talent for connecting to these stories stems from her life of research, life and professional experiences, farm life, college life, fortune 500 corporate management, spirituality, family, entrepreneurship, sales, genealogy, and publishing, to deliver relative multi-generational and multi-cultural products and services.

www.sulatoo.com

www.ingramcontent.com/pod-product-compliance
Lightning Source LLC
Chambersburg PA
CBHW070336120526
44590CB00017B/2904